Thank you...

... for purchasing this copy of Reading for Literacy for Reception. We hope that you find our materials helpful as part of your programme of literacy activities.

Please note that photocopies can only be made for use by the purchasing institution. Supplying copies to other schools, institutions or individuals breaches the copyright licence. Thank you for your help in this.

This Reading for Literacy book is part of our growing range of educational titles. Most of our books are individual workbooks but, due to popular demand, we are now introducing a greater number of photocopiable titles especially for teachers. You may like to look out for:

READING FOR LITERACY for ages 5-7, 7-8, 8-9, 9-10, 10-11

WRITING FOR LITERACY for ages 5-7, 7-8, 8-9, 9-10, 10-11

SPELLING FOR LITERACY for ages 5-7, 7-8, 8-9, 9-10, 10-11

NUMERACY TODAY for ages 5-7, 7-9, 9-11

HOMEWORK TODAY for ages 7-8, 8-9, 9-10, 10-11

BEST HANDWRITING for ages 7-11

To find details of our other publications, please visit our website: **www.acblack.com**

We hope that you have found this book useful. We would be very pleased to receive your comments on this book or to hear your suggestions for new books. If you wish to make any comments or if you would like to be put on our mailing list please contact us:

by telephone: **01480 212666**

by fax: **01480 405014**

by email: **sales@acblack.com**

by post: **A & C Black Publishers**
PO Box 19
St. Neots
Cambs
PE19 8SF

You may wish to photocopy and fax this page to us, completing any of the sections below that you feel relevant:

Name: ____

Address: ____

____

Telephone: ____

Email address: ____

Comments: ____

____

____

____

____

ABOUT THIS BOOK

The photocopiable pages in this book can be used individually but the book is designed to form 20 eight-page reading booklets that pupils can keep. These were developed by Chris Bell, the Headteacher of Oswestry Infant School and Nursery in Shropshire.

The booklets include the first 45 essential high frequency words. The focus words for each book are listed on the last page of each booklet. We have also provided large versions of the words at the back of the book. These can be photocopied on to Overhead Projector Transparencies or on to card to be used as flashcards. It is suggested that the Class Teacher, Learning Support Assistant or parent uses these focus words to play matching games, or uses magnetic letters to enhance the child's recognition of these words.

Additional words are used to make simple sentences and stories. Usually there are picture clues to help the child. Again, we have provided large versions of most of the additional words used.

Where possible, as part of the reading process, the child is asked to complete a simple task as a comprehension exercise e.g. 'Colour the ball' or 'Draw your teddy'. An adult should explain the task to the child.

We are grateful to the Department for Education and Skills for their permission to refer to the National Literacy Strategy.

NOTE
We suggest that the pages are removed and put in a ring binder for ease of use.

We have included a label to photocopy for the spine of your file. ➜

Andrew Brodie Publications

**Reading
for
Literacy
for
Reception**

Photocopiable
Sheets

www.acblack.com

Contents ...

A list of <u>some</u> of the additional words used in the books.

Where they are
first included.
BOOK

1. fish mouse snake
2. lion hippo zebra crocodile monkey
3. bike ball book
4. school teacher friend
5. party balloons presents cake ice-cream children
6. seaside fair
7. house car teddy
8. do what bike toys
9. park shops
10. zoo farm cow horse crab home
11. garden apples pears shop
12. pig duck with where sand bat
13. animals sleep frightened feed tiger elephant monkeys tired bed now
14. lost toy-box kitchen
15. sky fun helicopter air rocket plane
16. half-term holiday first train set next hide-and-seek town tomorrow
17. castle today moat help scared scary tower
18. hot cows sheep horses farmer nest hen pigs Sunday again
19. walk ran tree ladder
20. looked tea find grass bedroom

To make the booklets:

Photocopy both sides of the two A4 sheets that make up each booklet.

Fold them in half.

A long arm stapler can be used to fix them together if you wish.

Check that the pages are numbered correctly!

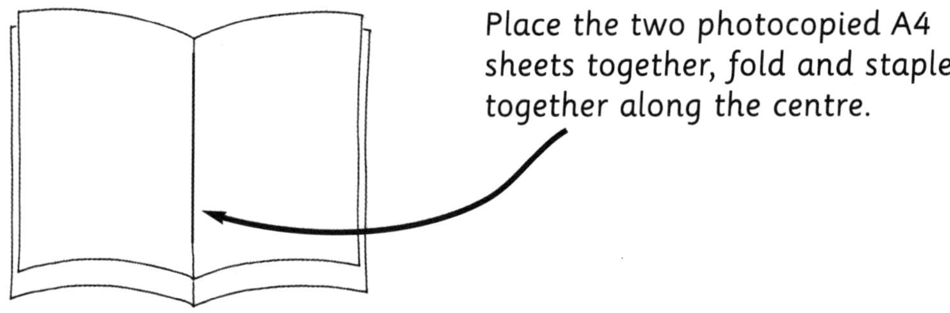

Place the two photocopied A4 sheets together, fold and staple together along the centre.

Book 1	I see a cat dog

These booklets have been designed to help children learn simple Key Words. Teachers use them in school. Enjoy reading them with your child. Make sure that you and your child point to each word as you read slowly. Please return this booklet to school every morning in the book bag.

I see a cat.

Name:

I see a cat.

Colour the cat.

I see a cat.

I see a dog.

I see a fish.

I see a mouse.

I see a snake.

I see a fish.

Colour the fish.

I see a mouse.

Colour the mouse.

I see a snake.

Colour the snake.

I see a dog.

Colour the dog.

Book 1	I see a cat dog
Book 2	can

These booklets have been designed to help children learn simple Key Words. Teachers use them in school. Enjoy reading them with your child. Make sure that you and your child point to each word as you read slowly. Please return this booklet to school every morning in the book bag.

I can see a lion.

Name:

I can see
a lion.

Draw a lion.

I can see a lion.

I can see a zebra.

I can see a crocodile.

I can see a monkey.

I can see a hippo.

Draw a hippo.

I can see a
hippo.

I can see a
zebra.

Draw a zebra.

I can see a crocodile.

Draw a crocodile.

I can see a monkey.

Draw a monkey.

Book 1	I see a cat dog
Book 2	can
Book 3	this is my mum

These booklets have been designed to help children learn simple Key Words. Teachers use them in school. Enjoy reading them with your child. Make sure that you and your child point to each word as you read slowly. Please return this booklet to school every morning in the book bag.

I can see my mum.

Name:

I can see my
mum.

I can see my mum.

I can see my bike.

I can see my dad.

This is my ball.

This is my book.

This is my dog.

This is my cat.

This
is my
dog.

Colour the dog.

This
is my
cat.

Colour the cat.

I can see my
bike.

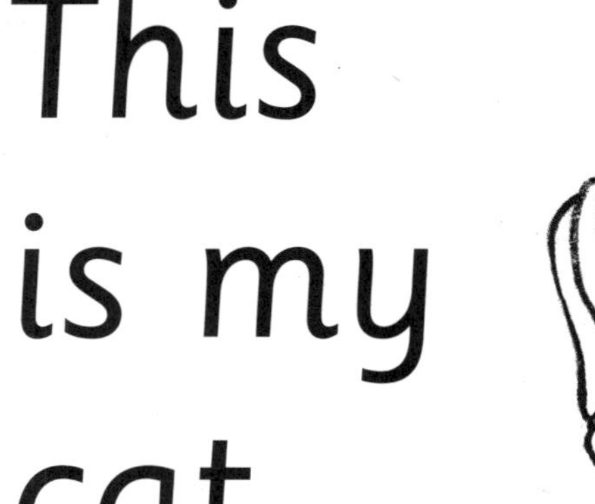

My bike.

This is my ball.

Colour the ball.

This is my book.

Colour the book.

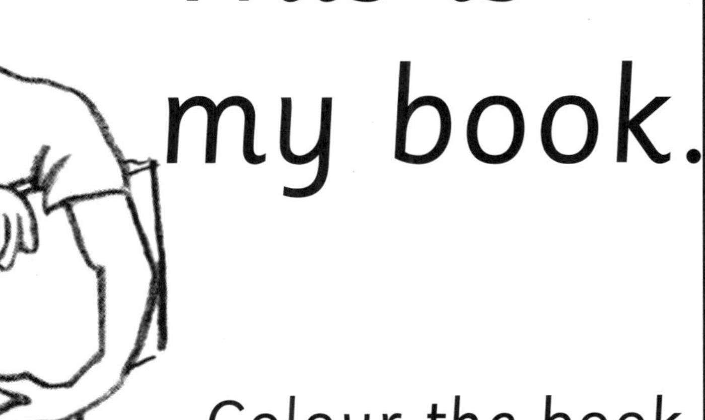

I can see my dad.

My dad.

Book 1	I see a cat dog
Book 2	can
Book 3	this is my mum
Book 4	like

These booklets have been designed to help children learn simple Key Words. Teachers use them in school. Enjoy reading them with your child. Make sure that you and your child point to each word as you read slowly. Please return this booklet to school every morning in the book bag.

I like my school.

Name:

I like my school.

Colour the school.

I like my school.

I can see my teacher.
I like my teacher.

My teacher likes me.

I can see my book.
I like my book.

I can see my friend.
I like my friend.

I can see my
friend.

I like my
friend.

Draw your friend.

I can see my
teacher.

I like my teacher.

Draw your teacher.

My teacher likes me.

I can see my book.

I like my book.

Book 1	I see a cat dog
Book 2	can
Book 3	this is my mum
Book 4	like
Book 5	the

These booklets have been designed to help children learn simple Key Words. Teachers use them in school. Enjoy reading them with your child. Make sure that you and your child point to each word as you read slowly. Please return this booklet to school every morning in the book bag.

The party

Name:

I can see the cake.

Colour the cake.

I can see the cake.

I like the ice-cream.

I can see the balloons.

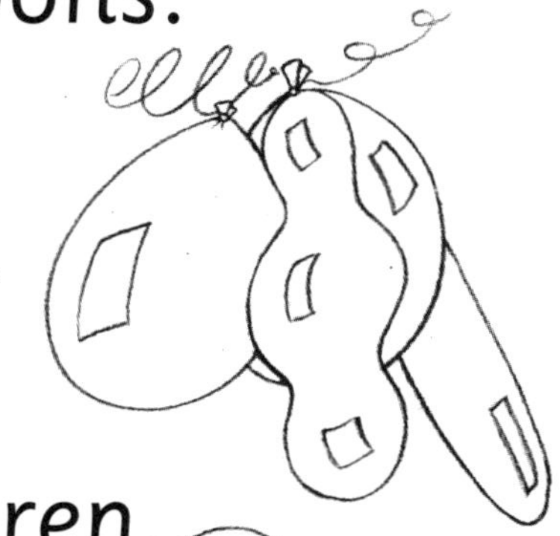

I like my presents.

I can see the children.

I can see the children.

Colour the children.

I like the ice-cream.

Draw an ice-cream.

I can see the balloons.

Colour the balloons.

I like my presents.

Colour the presents.

Book 6	went to

These booklets have been designed to help children learn simple Key Words. Teachers use them in school. Enjoy reading them with your child. Make sure that you and your child point to each word as you read slowly. Please return this booklet to school every morning in the book bag.

I went to the seaside.

Name:

I went to the seaside.

Draw yourself in the picture and colour it in.

I went to the seaside.

I went to the fair.

I went to a party.

The dog went to my house.

I went to the zoo.
I saw a hippo.

I went to the zoo.

I saw a hippo.

Colour the hippo.

I went to the fair.

Draw you in the picture
and colour it in.

I went to a party.

Colour the picture.

The dog went to my house.

Draw your house.

Book 6	went to
Book 7	can a see you yes

These booklets have been designed to help children learn simple Key Words. Teachers use them in school. Enjoy reading them with your child. Make sure that you and your child point to each word as you read slowly. Please return this booklet to school every morning in the book bag.

What can you see?

Name:

Can you see a dog?

Yes.

Colour the dog.

Can you see a dog?
Yes.

Can you see a cat?
Yes.

Can you see a house?
Yes.

Can you see a car?
Yes.

I can see my teddy.

I can see my teddy.

Draw your teddy.

Can you see a cat?

Yes.

Can you see a house?

Yes.

Draw your house.

Can you see a car?

Yes.

Draw another car.

Book 6	went　to
Book 7	can　a　see　you　yes
Book 8	my　I　like

These booklets have been designed to help children learn simple Key Words. Teachers use them in school. Enjoy reading them with your child. Make sure that you and your child point to each word as you read slowly. Please return this booklet to school every morning in the book bag.

What do I like?

Name:

I like my bike.

Draw your bike.

I like my bike.

I like my friend.

I like my teddy.

I can see my toys.

I like my toys.

I like my house.

Can I see my house?

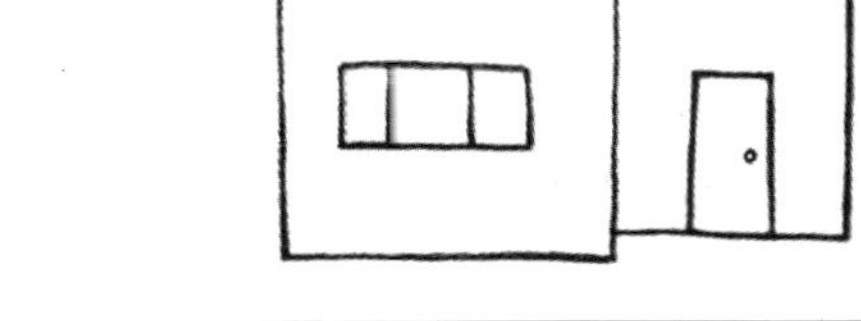

I like my house.

Can I see my house?

I like my friend.

Draw your friend.

I like my teddy.

Draw your teddy.

I can see the toys.

I like the toys.

Colour the toys.

Book 6	went to
Book 7	can a see you yes
Book 8	my I like
Book 9	the to went dad

These booklets have been designed to help children learn simple Key Words. Teachers use them in school. Enjoy reading them with your child. Make sure that you and your child point to each word as you read slowly. Please return this booklet to school every morning in the book bag.

I went to the park.

Name:

I went to the shops.

Colour the shops.

I went to the shops.

I went to the farm.
I saw a cow.

I went to the park.
I liked the park.

I went to the sea.
I saw a fish.

I went to my house.
I saw my dad.

I went to the farm.

I saw a cow.

I went to my house.

I saw my dad.

I went to the
park.

I liked the park.

I went to the
seaside.

I saw a fish.

Book 6	went to
Book 7	can a see you yes
Book 8	my I like
Book 9	the to went dad
Book 10	we go and

These booklets have been designed to help children learn simple Key Words. Teachers use them in school. Enjoy reading them with your child. Make sure that you and your child point to each word as you read slowly. Please return this booklet to school every morning in the book bag.

We go to the zoo.

The Zoo

Name:

We go to the park.

Draw yourself in the picture
and colour it in.

We go to the park.

We go to my house.

We go to the seaside.
I like the fish
and the crab.

We go to the farm.
I like the cow
and the horse.

We go to the zoo.
I can see a lion
and a monkey.

We go to the zoo.

I see a lion and a monkey.

We go to my house.

Draw your family in your home.

We go to the seaside.

I like the fish and the crab.

Colour the picture.

We go to the farm.

I like the cow and the horse.

Colour the picture.

Book 11	going am

These booklets have been designed to help children learn simple Key Words. Teachers use them in school. Enjoy reading them with your child. Make sure that you and your child point to each word as you read slowly. Please return this booklet to school every morning in the book bag.

I am going to school.

a b c
1 2 3

Name:

I am going to school.

Draw your school.

I am going to school.

I am going to the shop.

I like apples and pears.

I am going to the garden.
I can see my dog and cat.

I am going to the zoo.
I can see the lion
and the monkey.

I am going to the park.
I like the swings and
the slide.

I am going to the park.

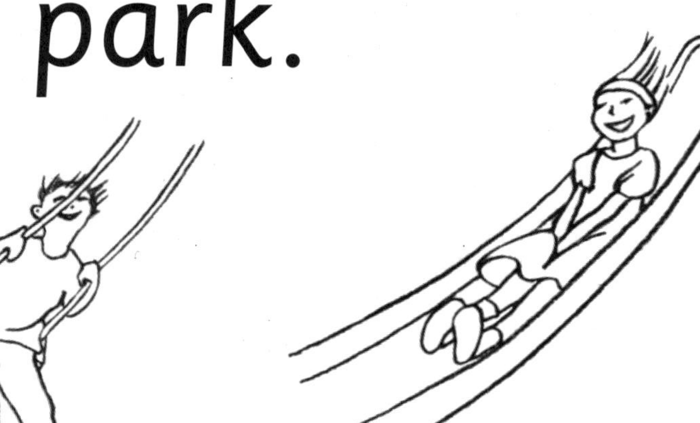

I like the swings and the slide.

Draw yourself in the park and colour the picture.

I am going to the shop.

I like apples and pears.

Draw 3 apples and 3 pears.

I am going to
the garden.

I can see my cat
and dog.

Colour the picture.

I am going to
the zoo.

I can see the lion
and the monkey.

Book 11	going am
Book 12	like go and play

These booklets have been designed to help children learn simple Key Words. Teachers use them in school. Enjoy reading them with your child. Make sure that you and your child point to each word as you read slowly. Please return this booklet to school every morning in the book bag.

Where can we go?

Name:

I go to the farm
and I can see a
pig and a duck.

Colour the picture.

I go to the farm and I can see
a pig and a duck.

I go to the park and I like the
swings and the slide.

We go to my house.
We can play with
my bike and my ball.

I go to the zoo and I like the
elephant and the crocodile.
I am going home.

We go to the seaside and
I play with the sand.

We go to the
seaside and I
play with the
sand.

Draw a sand castle.

I go to the park
and I like the
swings and the
slide.

We go to my house.

We play with my bat and my ball.

Colour the picture.

I go to the zoo and I like the elephant and the crocodile.

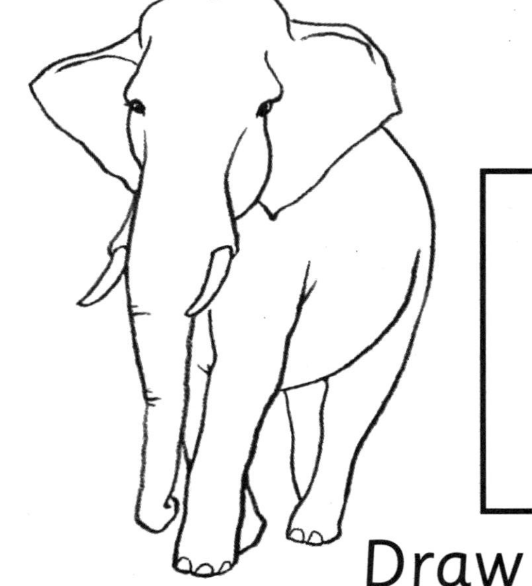

Draw an elephant.

Book 11	going am
Book 12	like go and play
Book 13	all said no yes

These booklets have been designed to help children learn simple Key Words. Teachers use them in school. Enjoy reading them with your child. Make sure that you and your child point to each word as you read slowly. Please return this booklet to school every morning in the book bag.

We went to the zoo.

Stories about

Name:

"We like animals. Can we go
to the zoo?"
"Yes," said Dad.

Sal and Taz and Mum and Dad
went to the zoo.

"I am tired," said Taz.
"Can we go home?"
"Yes," said Dad.

"You can go to bed now," said
Mum and Dad.
Good night Sal.
Good night Taz.

"Can you see all the monkeys?" said Mum.
"Yes," said Taz.

"I am going to feed the monkeys."
"No," said Mum.

Draw another monkey and colour the picture.

"I am going to see the snakes," said Sal.
"Can you see the red snake?" said Dad.

"Hisssssssss," said the snake and it went to sleep.

Draw a green snake and colour the picture.

"Can we go to see the tiger?"
said Sal.
"Yes…you can," said Dad.

"Grrrrrr," said the tiger.
"I am frightened," said Mum.

Draw a tiger cub and colour the picture.

"Can you see the elephant?"
said Taz.

"I am going to feed the elephant."
"No," said Dad.

Do you think Taz should feed the elephant?

Book 11	going am
Book 12	like go and play
Book 13	all said no yes
Book 14	in it is look big

These booklets have been designed to help children learn simple Key Words. Teachers use them in school. Enjoy reading them with your child. Make sure that you and your child point to each word as you read slowly. Please return this booklet to school every morning in the book bag.

Stories about

Where is Sal's teddy?

Name:

"Can you see my teddy?" said Sal.

"Oh no... my teddy is lost!" cried Sal.
"We can look in my bedroom," said Taz.

Colour the teddy.

Sal went to look in the garden.
"Can you see it?" said Taz.

"Yes, yes, yes!" shouted Sal.
"It is under the big tree."

Draw 4 apples on the tree and colour the picture.

"Go and look in the kitchen,"
said Taz.

"No - it is not in here."

How many pans are on the cooker?

Sal went into Taz's bedroom.
"Can you see it?"

"No," said Sal.
"You can look in the
bathroom," said Taz.

Can you see the teddy?

"Look in the bath," said Taz.

"I can see a duck and a frog...but no teddy."
"Where is it?" said Sal.

Draw a boat in the bath and colour the picture.

"You can look in my toy-box," said Taz.
"Is it there?"

"No," said Sal.
"My teddy is not in the box."

Colour the picture. How many toys are there in the box?

Book 11	going am
Book 12	like go and play
Book 13	all said no yes
Book 14	in it is look big
Book 15	was up on

These booklets have been designed to help children learn simple Key Words. Teachers use them in school. Enjoy reading them with your child. Make sure that you and your child point to each word as you read slowly. Please return this booklet to school every morning in the book bag.

Stories about

Holiday Adventures

Name:

Taz went up in a balloon.
It was fun.

"Look Sal...can you see me
up in the air?"

How many clouds are in the sky?

Sal and Taz were tired and
went home.

"You can go up to bed," said
Mum and Dad.
"Good night," said Taz and
Sal.
"It was an exciting holiday!"

Taz went on a fire-engine and
went up the ladder.
It was fun.

"Look - I am on the ladder,"
said Taz.
"Can I come up?" said Sal.

Sal went up in a helicopter.

It was exciting.
"Can you see me up in the
helicopter?" said Sal.

How many birds can you see?
Colour the picture.

Taz went up in a rocket.

"Can you see my rocket Sal?"

Count the stars and colour the picture.

Sal went on a plane.
The plane went up in the sky.

Sal was excited.

Draw the clouds in the sky and colour the picture.

Book 16	get play day at for

These booklets have been designed to help children learn simple Key Words. Teachers use them in school. Enjoy reading them with your child. Make sure that you and your child point to each word as you read slowly. Please return this booklet to school every morning in the book bag.

Stories about

The Half-Term Holiday

Name:

On the first day Taz and Sal went to play at a friend's house.

"We can play with the train set," said Sal.
It was fun.

How many children are playing with the train set?

On the last day, Taz and Sal went to play in the park.

"I like the park," said Sal.
It was time to go home.
"It is school tomorrow," said Dad.

The next day…Taz and Sal went for a ride on the bikes with Mum.

They went up a hill to play in the wood.

How many bikes are there? ☐
Colour the picture.

The next day…Tom and Sal went to town with Mum. It was boring.

"We can play hide and seek in the shop," said Taz. "No," said Mum.

Do Taz and Sal like shopping?

The next day…Taz and Sal went to play in the garden.

"Go and get the football," said Sal.
"No…it's too hot," said Taz.

The next day…Taz and Sal went to play up in Sal's tree-house.

"I like it up here," said Taz.
"It is fun."

Book 16	get play day at for
Book 17	they of at me she

These booklets have been designed to help children learn simple Key Words. Teachers use them in school. Enjoy reading them with your child. Make sure that you and your child point to each word as you read slowly. Please return this booklet to school every morning in the book bag.

Stories about

A Day at the Castle

Name:

"We can go to the castle today," said Dad.

They went in the car.
It was a sunny day.

How did they get to the castle?

They went up to the top of the tower.

At 5 o'clock it was time to go home.

They went in the dungeons.
It was scary.

"I am scared," said Taz.

Would you be scared in a dungeon?

At 12 o'clock they went to
the moat.

They had a picnic.
Sal had a bag of crisps.

What is Sal doing?

"I am going to feed the ducks," said Sal.

Dad went to help Sal.

What happened to Sal?

They went on the walls.

"Can you see me?" said Sal.

Colour the picture.

Book 16	get play day at for
Book 17	they of at me she
Book 18	day it on big

These booklets have been designed to help children learn simple Key Words. Teachers use them in school. Enjoy reading them with your child. Make sure that you and your child point to each word as you read slowly. Please return this booklet to school every morning in the book bag.

Stories about

A Day at the Farm

Name:

"We can go to the farm today," said Dad.

They went in the car.
It was a hot day.

"It is time to go home," said Dad.

"On no!" said Taz and Sal.
"We can go to the farm again on Sunday," said Mum.

"You can go to see the pigs,"
said Mum.

"Can we give them some of
the apples?" said Taz.
"Yes," said Mum.

They went to look at the cows
and sheep.

"Can I play with the cows?"
said Sal.
"No you can't," said Dad.

How many cows? ☐

How many sheep? ☐

They went to see the horses.

"You can ride on my horse,"
said the farmer.

Who is on the horse?

A big hen was on a nest.

"Is she going to have some
chicks?" said Sal.

How many hens are there?

Book 16	get play day at for
Book 17	they of at me she
Book 18	dog it on big
Book 19	away come she are

These booklets have been designed to help children learn simple Key Words. Teachers use them in school. Enjoy reading them with your child. Make sure that you and your child point to each word as you read slowly. Please return this booklet to school every morning in the book bag.

Stories about

A Cat and a Dog

Name:

"Please can I have a dog?" said Sal.

"Please can I have a cat?" said Taz.

"Yes," said Mum.

Have you got a pet?

Can my cat come up to bed with me?
Can my dog come up to bed with me?

"No!" said Mum. They have to sleep in the kitchen.
"Good night."

Next day they
went for a walk
with the dog.

The dog ran away.
They all ran after him.
Then they went home.

The next day they went to the
pet shop.

Taz and the cat went to play in a big tree.

"They are stuck," said Sal.

Mum got a ladder.

She went up the ladder to get them down.

Book 16	get play day at for
Book 17	they of at me she
Book 18	dog it on big
Book 19	away come she are
Book 20	he this she

These booklets have been designed to help children learn simple Key Words. Teachers use them in school. Enjoy reading them with your child. Make sure that you and your child point to each word as you read slowly. Please return this booklet to school every morning in the book bag.

Stories about

Taz and Sal play Hide-and-seek.

Name:

"Can we play hide and seek?"
said Sal.

"OK," said Dad.
"I will play with you."

Dad went into the garden.
He looked and he looked.

"You win!" said Dad. "Come
and have your tea now."

"It is my turn," said Sal.
"Come and find me in
the garden."

Taz went to look in the long
grass.
"Shhh - come and hide with
me," whispered Sal.

Sal hid in the wardrobe.
"Where is she?" said Taz.

"Look in the bedroom," said
Dad.
"She is in the wardrobe!"

Taz went in the garden.
He hid in the tree-house.

"Look - he is in the tree-house," said Dad.
"This is fun," said Sal.

"I am going to hide now," said Dad. "Come and find me!"

"I can see him," said Taz.
"He is behind the curtain!"

I	up
look	we
like	and
on	at
for	he

is	said
go	you
are	this
going	they
away	play

a	am
cat	to
come	day
the	dog
big	my

mum	no
dad	all
get	in
went	was
of	me

she

see

it

yes

can

The following words also appear within the set of books.

fish

bike

ball

book

mouse

snake

zebra

monkey

crocodile

lion

friend

school

teacher

party

cake

balloons

presents

ice-cream

children

seaside

fair house

car	teddy
do	what
where	toys
park	shop
zoo	farm

cow

horse

crab

home

garden

apples

pears

shops

pig	duck
do	what
with	sand
yourself	
bat	sleep

feed

tiger

tired

bed

animals

frightened

now

lost

elephant

monkeys

toy-box

kitchen

sky

fun

Words used in the books

air | plane

rocket

helicopter

half-term

holiday

first

next

train set

hide-and-seek

tomorrow

today

town

castle

moat

help

scary

scared

Sunday

tower

hot

cows

sheep

horses

farmer

nest

hen

pigs

again

walk

ran

tree

tea

looked

ladder

find

grass